The approaching view of the Bowes Museum in County Durham. The museum houses an important collection of North Country quilts.

A thatched cottage on the main street of the village of Adair, Ireland. Adair is called one of Ireland's most picturesque villages.

ACROSS THE POND

PROJECTS INSPIRED BY QUILTS OF THE BRITISH ISLES

BY BETTINA HAVIG

Across the Pond

Projects Inspired by Quilts of the British Isles

By Bettina Havig

EDITOR: Deb Rowden

DESIGNER: Kelly Ludwig

PHOTOGRAPHY: Aaron T. Leimkuehler

ILLUSTRATION: Eric Sears

TECHNICAL EDITOR: Kathe Dougherty

PRODUCTION ASSISTANCE: Jo Ann Groves

TRAVEL PHOTOS: Bettina Havig

PUBLISHED BY: KANSAS CITY STAR BOOKS
1729 Grand Blvd.
Kansas City, Missouri, USA 64108

First edition, first printing
ISBN: 978-1-935362-20-3

Library of Congress Control Number: 2009931385

Printed in the United States of America by Walsworth Publishing Co., Marceline, MO

To order copies, call StarInfo at (816) 234-4636 and say "Books."

PickleDish.com
The Quilter's Home Page

www.PickleDish.com

A visitor enjoys the sights of the Beamish Open Air Museum, which recreates a small industrial village of the early 20th century, a quiet time just prior to World War I.

TABLE OF CONTENTS

PROJECTS

Acknowledgements

Aside from the many friends and colleagues who assisted in this book I owe a debt of gratitude to the anonymous quilt makers of the British Isles who over the past 200 years have made the quilts that will inspire today's quiltmakers to continue the traditions. How I wish I could have met some of them.

Thanks to my long-suffering family through all the preparation for the book including all the times I was off enjoying the delights of the British Isles without them.

In the British Isles there are several people who generously spent time and offered expertise about quilts and arranged for me to see quilts. Among them are Diane Huck, Dorothy Osler, Lynne Edwards, Sheilah Daughtree, Rosemary Allen, and Judy Mendelssohn in the UK and Emer Fahy and Maeve Meany in Ireland.

Thank you to my editors Deb Rowden who nurtured the text and me; Kathe Dougherty who edited the technical side to try to keep us all out of trouble; Aaron Leimkuehler who made the quilts smile as soon as he said 'cheese'; and Kelly Ludwig, who turned all of the notes, photos and graphics into a lovely book, and Eric Sears, who turned my near-stick figures into real illustrations.

ABOUT THE AUTHOR

Bettina Havig has been quilting since 1970 and teaching since 1974. Bettina is a quiltmaker, teacher, lecturer, judge, quilt historian, and consultant. She has taught for guilds throughout the US as well as in Spain, Ireland, Wales, Germany, England, and Scotland. In 2008, Bettina was the featured quilter of the Spanish Patchwork Association annual conference.

She has been an active member of the American Quilt Study Group since 1980 and presented a paper on the findings of the Missouri Heritage Quilt Project at their annual seminar in 1986. Bettina served as President of AQSG from 2002 to 2006 and represented AQSG on the advisory board of the International Quilt Study Center in Lincoln, NE, 2002-2006.

Her work has been featured in *American Patchwork and Quilting, Quilters' Newsletter Magazine, Quilt, Lady's Circle Patchwork, Traditional Quiltworks, Quilting Today, Sew Many Quilts,* and Fons and Porter's *Love of Quilting*. She was featured in both the British *Patchwork and Quilting* and the French *Quilt Mania* magazines.

This is her first Kansas City Star book: she has written six other books.

Bettina is active in her local quilt guild in Columbia, MO and was founding chairman of the Missouri State Quilters' Guild. She serves on the national advisory board for collections and on the board of trustees for the National Quilt Museum (formerly MAQS) in Paducah, KY. She also serves on the board of the International Quilt Study Center in Lincoln, NE. Bettina maintains a busy travel and teaching schedule throughout the year, which helps her stay current on quilts and quilt values. She is preparing an exhibit of Amish crib quilts as guest curator for the New England Quilt Museum opening January, 2010.

WELCOME TO THE WORLD OF BRITISH ISLES QUILTS

The British Isles are the source of our greatest heritage of quilt making. The techniques and styles of British quilts and British fabrics greatly influenced the early quilt makers in America in the 18th and 19th centuries. The earliest style, which we call Medallion quilts were more frequently referred to as Frame quilts. They reflect a style of framing a center focus block with a sequence of borders or "frames". The Strippy quilts in the book might be called Bars quilts in the US but they are a popular and often used format for British quilts in the 19th and early 20th centuries. They most often were just the long strips combined to span the space but could and did sometimes include pieced blocks within the strips.

Patchwork and quilting are actually often talked about separately while here they are somewhat interchangeable terms. We are less likely to distinguish one from the other. Patchwork, especially in the 19th century in Britain, was often done over a paper template. That is sometimes referred to as English template piecing. The more recent term is mosaic because the technique is not limited to England. The process is multi-stepped beginning with a paper shape for each piece of fabric. The fabric, which was not necessarily carefully cut to shape, was wrapped over the template, basted in place and then sewn to the other similarly prepared pieced with an overcast or ladder stitch.

As paper was a scarcer commodity for early American quilt makers it wasn't long before the paper was abandoned and the pieces cut to shape and sewed together with a running stitch.

Quilting was not always done over the patchwork top after completion. Some quilts or coverlets were never quilted, only backed to protect the raw edges of the small component pieces of fabric. Something called a coverlet was less likely to be quilted.

A classic Victorian hotel in Leominster, England.

Quilting on the other hand might have been done to complete a quilt but was also popular in its own right. Many British quilts are 'wholecloth'. No patchwork at all. Or simply long vertical strips sewed together to result in a top large enough for use as a bed cover. The wholecloth quilting traditional was kept alive by a handful of quilters in the last half of the 20th century, most notably Amy Emms.

Regardless of which techniques were employed to make the top, the quilting motifs are distinctive from American quilt motifs with only a few basic motifs being used on both American and British quilts. Cables and feathered motifs were popular choices on both sides of the Atlantic.

Quilts were rarely bound with a separate binding. The finish seen most frequently is a 'knife edge' or slip stitched finish where the layers are turned in at the edges and slip stitched closed.

The projects in this book will give you a taste of the styles used in quilts from "Across the Pond". Quilting motifs are included to give you options to make your quilt more like the traditional quilts of the British Isles. Irish quilts fall snugly into the tradition. They are often not as sophisticated but they are all the more interesting in a way. Welsh quilts that are frequently made of wool can resemble our Amish quilts. It makes us stop to ponder what the connection might be.

The quilts' names conjure up memories of places and experiences from my trips to England, Wales, Scotland and Ireland.

I hope that you will enjoy making some or all of the quilts here. I would love to see photos of any quilts made from the projects in the book. What greater compliment could I have?

SCOTLAND

IRELAND

•Limerick

ENGLAND

Beamish•

St. John's Chapel•

Berrington
Hall•   •Worcester

St. Ives•   •Bildeston

•Abergavenny

London•

My Romance with the Quilts of the British Isles

Why me... why would a quiltmaker from central Missouri develop such an interest in and knowledge of quilts made thousands of miles away and so many years ago?

Well…

In 1989 I met Dorothy Osler. Dorothy is a quilt historian in the UK. She had been invited to speak at a retreat in Northern California at a magical place called Pt. Bonita. We became immediate friends. Two years later when I was preparing to curate an exhibition of contemporary British quilts, I enlisted Dorothy's assistance.

I flew to London in 1991 and was met by Annette Claxton, a London area quiltmaker, who had arranged for me to speak to a group of suburban London quiltmakers. Within days I boarded a train for Edinburgh to conduct workshops and lectures in Scotland and later in County Durham, Northumberland. All the while I was meeting quilters and scouting for quilts for the exhibition at the National Quilt Festival.

This was the beginning of my ongoing love of the history of the British and Irish quilts and a passion for the style of their early quilts. I maneuvered my way into the set up day for Quilts UK to look for more quilts for the exhibition. In the process I met Dianne Huck, editor of *British Patchwork and Quilting* magazine. Some years later I found myself back in Malvern to judge Quilts UK in 1998.

These historic quilts appeal to me for several reasons. I love the history of the early textiles and quilts. I am strongly attracted to the frame or medallion style and to the luscious fabrics from which these early quilts were made. I am a "quilter" so the variations in quilting motifs spoke volumes to me. Who knows, I may have been a dedicated quiltmaker in a former life a century and half ago and continent away. The earliest extant English quilts date to the mid 18th century. That's comparable to our American traditions but the differences and similarities are fascinating. The early quilts of the British Isles show striking influences on our early 19th century quilts. Now our quilt styles are influencing contemporary quilts there.

BRITAIN

I always rent a car while in Britain. How else could I wander the countryside, prowling for antique sewing tools and seeing wonderful old quilts? Needless to say, by now I was completely enamored of the quilts. Subsequent trips, there can never be too many, have taken me to many parts of England, Scotland, Wales, and Ireland. The rental car, or hired car as the English say, enabled me to take spontaneous side trips. I could get to out of the way places that would have been so hard to access on public transport… if I could get there at all. The car was like a magic carpet that took me to an antique faire in Ludlow, to the quilts and christening gown exhibit in St. John's Chapel (a village not a church), to the Beamish Open Air Museum and the Bowes Museum, to the Harris Museum in Preston, to Lucy Boston's home in Hemingford Grey, to the Forge Needle Museum in Redditch, and to so many other sites.

The generous people I met in the many visits have opened doors that otherwise I wouldn't even have known about. In casual conversations, they might mention a place or event. I would whip out my trusty British driving atlas and plot my way for the day. I have been to large and small museums, local quilt shows, guild meetings and National Trust properties all in the cause of learning more about British quilts. Of course, I had a lovely time along the way.

IRELAND

In 2006, I was invited to be the primary instructor for the annual conference weekend of the Quilters Guild of Ireland. I arrived through Shannon airport, spent the night with a friend in Limerick and then off to the conference the next morning. We had to drive to the site of the weekend conference held in Ballybofey near Donegal, nearly the length of the country away. The mileage of about 220 is less the issue than the roads - often very narrow, hilly and winding - so the journey took most of the day. I made the drive in the company of Emer Fahy, an authority on Irish quilt history; we had loads of time to talk. She has been a wonderful resource for information on Irish quilts. The Irish quilts that I have seen bear common elements with the Welsh and English quilts however the materials may differ.

WALES

Judy Mendelsohhn, a Welsh quilter and friend, connected me with quilters in Wales for an evening talk about American quilters (while I listened intently for anything I could learn about Welsh quilts). Through Judy a trip to Jen Jones shop in Llanybydder, West Wales was arranged. Even with a Welsh quilter along, the shop was hard to find! Jen Jones has collected and sold quilts, specializing in Welsh quilts for many years. We had the run of the shop to look at dozens and dozens of 19th and 20th century quilts (actually she says a thousand). While her shop is not a museum, it contains more quilts and variety of quilts than you can find in several museums. It was a comprehensive lesson in the styles and composition of Welsh quilts.

The experiences and the exposure to the quilts has always been pure pleasure. I will forever be grateful to so many who have shared during my six trips there. And I will go back to the British Isles for more quilt related experiences just as often as I can. I recommend it to you.

The project instructions in this book assume a basic understanding of quilting techniques. There are many wonderful instruction books available: please refer to your favorite for detailed how-to information.

FRAME QUILTS

In British vernacular "Frame" quilts are what American quiltmakers call Medallion quilts. Each sequence of borders that make up a Medallion quilt is a sequence of 'frames'. In deference to the historic style, we will call our borders frames throughout this book. As you construct and add frames you will be adding the sequence of borders. Enjoy the projects.

PROJECTS

The view of the grounds from the steps of the Bowes Museum near Barnard Castle, County Durham.

Beamish Strippy Quilt

51" x 62 1/4"

In 1991, I made my first trip to the United Kingdom to scout quilts for an American exhibition. My friend and colleague Dorothy Osler took me to the Beamish Open Air Museum (beamish.org.uk), where I tasted the history of the area and the wonderful collection housed there. The Beamish tells the story of folks from the northeastern area of England at two important periods: 1825, and the years leading up to World War I. Those pre war years are when the inspiration quilt for this project was made.

The Beamish museum is located just a few miles from both Newcastle and Durham in County Durham. The inspiration quilt is a simple strippy quilt, much like many made in this style. In 2004, I returned to the Beamish to study their quilt notebooks and photos and I saw approximately 30 quilts that were on display... in fact, they held the quilts one day longer than planned so that a friend and I could see them. That lovely day was facilitated by Dorothy and graciously granted by Rosemary Allen, curator.

So it is appropriate that this is the first project in this book.

Lillian Hedley, a well respected quilt teacher, made this reproduction of a quilt in the Beamish Open Air Museum collection. The original quilt is circa 1870-1880.

Hints for Choosing Fabrics

For the strips, select a striped fabric with narrow repeats. Choose a floral that will set the palette for the Four Patches and that works well with your stripe.

The fabrics for the Four Patch units should be prints but read as solids.

Yardage Requirements

- » 1 7/8 yards of a striped fabric
- » 1 7/8 yards of a medium scale floral print (includes binding)
- » 1/4 yard each of 3 medium to dark prints that coordinate with the floral and stripe
- » 1/4 yard each of 3 light prints in the same color families as the medium to dark prints
- » 1/2 yard of a light background print
- » 4 yards backing/lining
- » 56" x 67" batting

Construction

Four Patch units

From each 1/4 yard print for the Four Patches:

Cut

- » 2 strips 2 1/2" wide across the width of the fabric
- » Sew a medium/dark strip to a light strip of the same color. Repeat for 2 strip sets of each colorway.
- » Press seams to the darker fabric in each strip.

- » Slice the strips into 2 1/2" wide cuts.

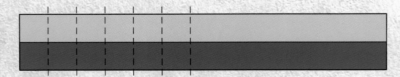

- » Sew 12 Four Patch blocks of each color group.

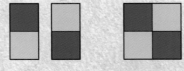

From the background fabric

Cut
- » 10 - 7" squares, subcut twice on the diagonal, for 40 triangles.
- » 6 - 3 3/4" squares, subcut once on the diagonal for 12 triangles.

Construct the pieced strips
- » Randomly place 11 Four Patch units in each panel/strip; vary the positions. Trim and true the corners and sides to 1/4" seam allowance.

An early 19th century manor house, not grand by English standards but by local standards. The manor is part of the surrounds of Beamish Open Air Museum.

For the strippy panels

» Cut 2 - 6 1/8" x 62 3/4" strips from the floral print.
» Cut 4 panels 6 1/8" wide x 62 3/4" from your striped fabric.
» Mark the reverse side of the 2 center strippy panels that join to the Four Patch panels for alignment. Draw a line across the strip at each Four Patch interval so that the blocks line up across the quilt.
» Sew the panels together, left to right, pressing the seams away from the pieced panels.

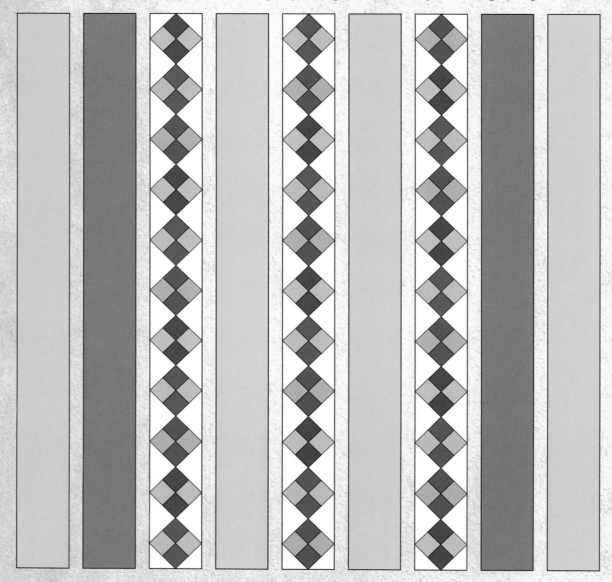

Stripe, floral, four patch, stripe, four patch, stripe, four patch, floral, stripe

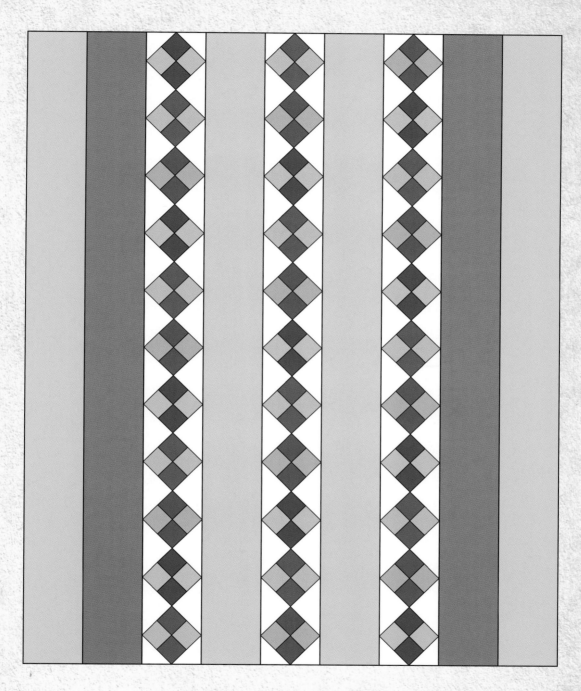

Finishing

The cable design for the quilting of the center stripes is found on pg 87.

ABERGAVENNY WELSH QUILT

60" x 60"

On my trip to the UK in 2008 I made a three-day side excursion and visited Jen Jones quilt shop in south Wales, thanks to arrangements made by friends. Jen has amassed an impressive private quilt collection and also has many, many quilts for sale. I saw several quilts reminiscent of traditional Welsh quilts and several quite similar to Amish quilts found in the USA.

On an earlier visit to England I attended a quilt exhibition at the American Museum at Bath. Its focus was a comparison of Welsh and Amish quilts. Many of those Welsh quilts were from Jen Jones's collection.

On still another trip I viewed more Welsh quilts at the Needle Forge Museum in Reddich, a primary supplier of needles. There I saw and photographed the inspiration quilt for Abergavenny Welsh quilt. Both the maker of my inspiration quilt and the current owner are unknown. The name reflects that pleasant trip to Wales. Abergavenny is known as the gateway to south Wales.

The medallion center of this wool Welsh quilt is an Evening Star. The style calls to mind the Amish quilts found in the eastern United States.

Yardage Requirements

This quilt would have been made in wool, like wool challis or wool broadcloth. Since those options are not practical for this project, it is made in cotton flannel.

* For the frames, cut the longest frames first and work back to the shortest and the squares. Cut frame 4 first, then 3, and 1 before cutting for the pieced frame.

- » 2 yards black
- » 1 3/8 yards gray
- » 3/4 yard forest green
- » 3/4 yard red
- » 1/4 yard bright blue
- » 4 yards backing (includes binding)
- » 64" x 64" batting

Cutting

For the Evening Star in the center cut
- » 1 - 10 1/2" square red
- » 4 - 5 7/8" squares red, subcut once on the diagonal
- » 4 - 5 1/2" squares forest green
- » 1 - 11 1/4" square forest green, subcut twice on diagonal

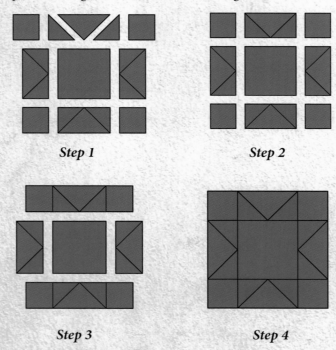

Step 1   *Step 2*

Step 3   *Step 4*

The block should measure 20" finished.

Frame 1:

Plain with cornerstones cut
- » 4 - 5 1/2" squares gray
- » 4 - 5 1/2" x 20 1/2" strips black

Frame 2:

Sawtooth cut
- » 4 - 5 1/2" squares black
- » 12 - 5 7/8" squares red, subcut once on the diagonal
- » 12 - 5 7/8" squares forest green, subcut once on the diagonal

Subcut the squares.

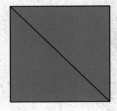

You need 24 Sawtooth units.

Frame 3:

Plain with cornerstones cut
- » 4 - 5 1/2" squares bright blue
- » 4 - 5 1/2" x 40 1/2" strips gray

Frame 4:

Plain with cornerstones cut
- » 4 - 5 1/2" squares red
- » 4 - 5 1/2" x 50 1/2" black

Assembly Diagram

Construction

Place the star in the center as shown above.

Frame 1

Sew black frame strips to each side of the center star.

Sew a gray square to each end of the remaining black frame strips and, matching the seam at the corners of the star, sew the borders to the top and bottom of the center panel.

Frame 2

Assemble the Sawtooth units. Sew 6 Sawtooth units together for each side, top, and bottom of the quilt. Attach the side borders to the center panel with the red triangles toward the center as shown. Sew the corner squares onto the remaining sets of 6 Sawtooth units for the top and bottom. Press toward the inner frame.

Frame 3

Attach the gray frame strips to the sides of the quilt. Sew the bright blue squares to each end of the remaining frame strips and attach to the top and bottom of the quilt. Press toward the gray frame.

Frame 4

Sew the black frame strips to the side of the quilt. Sew the corner squares to each end of the final 2 black strips. Attach to the top and bottom of the quilt. Press to the outside.

Finishing

Suggested quilting motifs are on page 88.

Traditionally Welsh quilts are bound with a 'knife edge," meaning no binding shows on the front of the quilt. That edge is very difficult to keep straight and even. This quilt is bound to simulate that style. Cut binding strips from the same fabric as the backing, 1 1/2" wide, join the strips; you will need about 250" of binding. (6 or 7 strips joined). Attach the first side of the binding to the front of the quilt as usual using a 1/4" seam allowance. Turn the entire binding to the back of the quilt. Turn under half the width and hand stitch with a blind stitch to the back, mitering at the corners as you go around the quilt.

A charming view of the river winding along the edge of Adair.

A Nod to Amy

A whole cloth decorative European style pillow sham
26" x 26"

A Nod to Amy honors and remembers Amy Emms MBE*, who taught quilting and fostered and preserved traditional quilting techniques used in Northumberland, an area in the north of England. Amy lived in a village called St. Johns Chapel. On a trip to Barnard Castle, County Durham we visited an antique shop on the high street. When the proprietor discovered our interest in English quilts she directed us to an exhibition of quilts and christening gowns being held that weekend in St. Johns Chapel. In our naiveté we at first thought it was a church. It was, in fact, Amy Emms' village. Amy died in 1998 shortly after the annual Quilts UK show where I had the privilege of meeting her. She was always on hand for the final day of the show to award the prizes. Amy was held in great esteem. Whole cloth quilts are an important genre of quilts in the English tradition.

MBE stands for Member of the British Empire, a special honor given to those who have made significant contributions in their field of concentration.

An example of whole cloth crib or cot quilt at Jen Jones shop in Wales.

Amy Emms, a gracious English quilter who helped sustain the quilting traditions of the north of England.

Yardage Requirements

» 1 7/8 yards of solid color for outer sham. Note: I used sateen, which was very popular for use in whole cloth quilts in the first part of the 20th century especially in the North of England. You may use any solid color desired.

» 1 yard backing for the quilted top of the sham

» 30" x 30" batting

The quilting motif for your whole cloth sham is a traditional North Country design known as "Scissors".

» Cut a 28" x 28" square for the top of the sham. Center and mark the design on the square using a light box to trace it onto the square or use a template (see page xx for the design, which will be repeated 4 times). Fold the square in half on both the straight and diagonal and crease lightly. That divides the square into 8 sections. Position the design, centered, on the sections. Draw a 3 3/4" circle to help with placement.

» *Note:* The light box allows the design to be traced even through dark fabric such as my choice of eggplant purple.

» Baste the top, batting, and lining together. Quilt the pattern, then fill all the background areas including the area in the center with a grid of quilting. I used 1/2" crosshatching in the center and double rows of crosshatching in the rest of the background.

» Trim the square to 27" x 27" and stay-stitch the outside edge.

To complete the 26" x 26" sham:

» Cut 2 pieces of the matching fabric, each 17 1/2" x 27" for the back of the sham.

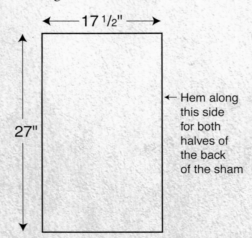

» Along one 17 1/2" side of each back piece, turn under 1/4". Press and then turn under a 2" hem and top stitch. Overlap the 2" hems of each half completely and

baste them together along the overlapping hems. The back should measure 27" x 27".
Measure the backing and trim to 27" x 27" if necessary. Now you can treat the back
as a single piece. After the sham is complete, remove the basting so you can insert the
purchased European pillow or the pillow form you've made.

» With right side of the whole cloth top facing the right side of the back, stitch all the
way around the sham using a 1/2" seam allowance. To reinforce the seam, stitch
around a second time about 1/4" out. Remove the basting, turn the sham right side
out and insert the pillow or pillow form.

Note: You may use the whole cloth design on any square or rectangle that is at least 16" in
either dimension, that is, for a standard bed pillow or decorative throw pillow.

See pages 89-90 for the pattern.

Berrington Hall Medallion Quilt

74" x 74"

Berrington Hall is a National Trust site, a fine manor house that is open to visitors. It is just north of Leominister in Worcestershire. The staff discovered an early 19th century frame quilt hidden away in a window seat. There is no provenance for the quilt but English quilt historians have dated the quilt to circa 1820-30 by comparing fabrics of known vintage to those in the quilt. A friend, Sheilah Daughtree, who is researching the quilt arranged for us to see it, ponder over it, and enjoy the rich array of early fabrics. For dessert following that luscious quilt, we had our lunch in the tearoom on the grounds of the manor house. It was a delightful day in spite of a predictable English downpour.

The center of this quilt is a 14" medallion. Use a printed panel or construct any center of your choice. If your panel or printed square is smaller than 14" finished, add a small frame to enlarge it to the 14" finished size.

Note: To avoid piecing plain borders, cut the longest plain borders first, working back to the shortest plain borders.

A frame quilt found in a window seat at Berrington Hall. The quilt takes its name from the fabric used in the center medallion, a decorator fabric featuring a pineapple. Photo by Sheilah Daughtree.

Yardage requirements

- » 2 1/4 yards of theme or focus fabric for frames/borders and binding
- » 2 yards of light or medium light prints, mixers
- » 3 yards of dark and medium dark prints, mixers
- » 4 1/4 yards for the backing
- » 76" x 76" batting

Use an assortment of prints, at least six or more different prints for the light and dark ranges. The more prints you use, the more pleasing the finished quilt will be. Most of the piecing and frames (borders) are quilted with straight lines. For the center medallion; use any 14 1/2" panel, printed square, or pieced or appliquéd block of your choice.

Cutting

Frame 1:

Sawtooth:

Select 1 light and 1 medium print from your assortment, cut

- » 28 - 2 7/8" squares of light prints
- » 28 - 2 7/8" squares of medium/dark prints

Subcut the squares once along the diagonal and assemble 28 Sawtooth units.

For the corners of frame 1 cut

An assortment of 8 - 2 7/8" squares, subcut diagonally. Piece 4 Sawtooth units for the corners.

Frame 2:

Plain, theme/focus fabric cut
- » 2 - 2 3/4" x 18 1/2" strips
- » 2 - 2 3/4" x 23" strips

Frame 3:

Hour Glass units, you need 48 units.

From the entire assortment of prints, cut at least 44 total 3 1/2" squares. Subcut on both diagonals and assemble 44 Hour Glass units, mixing the fabrics for good variety.

Cut

> » 48 - 3 1/2" squares.

Frame 4:

A plain, theme/focus fabric, cut

> » 2 - 3 1/2" x 27 1/2" strips
> » 2 - 3 1/2" x 33 1/2" strips

Frame 5:

Framed squares, you need 44 framed square units and 4 Double Four Patch units at the corners.

For the framed squares cut

> » 44 - 3 1/2" squares from an assortment of your mixers. (You may want to cut more to increase the variety in the combinations.)
> » 176 - 2" squares

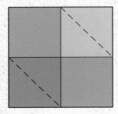

> » Stitch a 2" square to each corner. Trim away the excess triangles and press.

For the Four Patch corners cut

> » 16 - assorted 2" squares and make 4 Four Patch units.

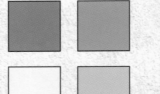  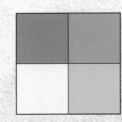

Frame 6:

Plain border, focus/theme fabric, cut
- » 2 - 2 1/4" x 39 1/2"
- » 2 - 2 1/4" x 43"

Frame 7:

Triple-squares.

Use as much variety as possible. You need 80 triple square-units and 4 turning units.

Cut
- » 176 - 2" squares, medium/dark
- » 88 - 2" squares, light
- » 44 - 2 3/4" squares, subcut on both diagonals

Subcut 3 1/2" squares diagonally twice.

Each unit consists of a triangle 3 - 2" squares and another triangle.
Stitch the unit together.

Align the units as shown, offsetting by 1 square. Stitch together. Trim edges if needed — the finished strip should be 4 3/4" wide.

Turning unit construction. This unit completes the frame.

36

Frame 8:

Plain, focus fabric, cut

- » 2 - 2" x 51 1/2"
- » 2 - 2" x 54 1/2"

Frame 9:

Framed Squares.

You will need 36 units. The corners are double Four Patch units.

For the Framed Squares cut

- » 36 - 6 1/2" squares
- » 144 – 3 1/2" squares

Construct the framed squares as shown in Frame 5 on page 35.

For the corners cut

- » 32 - 2" squares, assorted fabrics
- » 8 - 3 1/2" squares, assorted fabrics

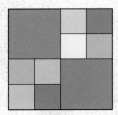

Frame 10:

Plain, focus fabric with a plain square at the corners, any fabric, cut

- » 4 - 4 1/2" x 66 1/2"
- » 4 - 4 1/2" squares for corners

Construction

Work from the center medallion out. Construct each group of units. Join the necessary number of units to make the border strips. Add the frame to the sides in each sequence first, then attach the top and bottom frames or borders. Only frame 7 has a mitered corner. The corner units make the miter.

Assembly Diagram

Finishing

Quilting motifs for Berrington Hall are grids and combinations of straight line quilting. Grids of all sorts are used commonly on English quilts along with variations of our traditional feathers and cables or what might be called 'twists'.

Binding

Cut 9 strips 1 3/4" wide across the grain, selvage to selvage. Join the strips so you have at least 320" of binding. Fold the binding in half and press. This doubles the thickness of the binding for better wear. Trim the quilt and attach the binding to the front of the quilt using a 1/4'" seam allowance. Turn to the back and slip stitch in place.

Berrington Hall with a friend and myself on the steps.

BILDESTON UNEVEN NINE PATCH QUILT

34" x 51"

Bildeston is the home village of a very important English quilt teacher, Lynne Edwards, who has recently been named MBE*. It's a quiet village in Suffolk but one with a very active quilting community. Naming the quilt for the village is really a tip of the hat to Lynne. Suffolk is in the East of England, known for 'Suffolk' pink thatched roof houses. Lynne lives in a 900-year-old house right on the high street**. It's tiny, cozy, and charming.

This is one of the earliest block designs found in quilts, including those of the British Isles. It's a simple design to construct and very effective on point.

*MBE stands for Member of the British Empire, a special honor given to those who have made significant contributions in their field of concentration

**The high street in any town or village is the main thoroughfare, where most businesses are located in smaller towns. It's their Main Street.

I couldn't resist a photo of Simple Simon's pie shop across the diamond of Donegal. The Donegal town square is shaped like a diamond.

Yardage Requirements

For the pieced Uneven Nine Patch blocks:

  » 8-10 1/4 yard or fat quarters of light prints and 6-8 1/4 yard of medium-dark to dark prints.

For alternate blocks and binding:

  » 1 7/8 yards of medium to large scale print, medium or dark. Reserve 1/3 yard for binding.
  » 1 5/8 yards backing
  » 38" x 55" batting (crib size)

Cutting

  » There are 24 - 6" finished Uneven Nine Patch blocks.
  » Use as many combinations of the light and dark prints as you want.

For each block cut

  » 4 - 2" x 3 1/2" rectangles of medium to dark fabric
  » 1 - 3 1/2"x 3 1/2" square of light fabric
  » 4 - 2" x 2" squares of light fabric

For the Setting units cut

15 - 6 1/2" x 6 1/2" squares

4 - 9 3/4" x 9 3/4" squares, subcut on both diagonals (yields 16 triangles) for sides

2 - 5 1/8" x 5 1/8" squares, subcut on the diagonal once for the corners

Construction

Set the blocks in diagonal rows. Add corners, and end caps to each diagonal row as you go.

Finishing

For quilting motifs for the alternate blocks and border, see page 91.

» Cut 1 3/4" strips for binding. Stitch the strips together using diagonal seams, fold in half and press for doubled binding.

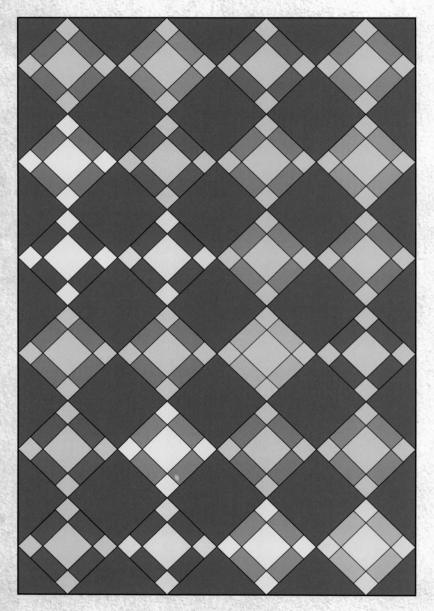

Assembly Diagram

Jen Jones quilt shop is housed in what must have been a small farm cottage. Many of the quilts were displayed on the upper floor, reached by something more like a ladder than stairs. But the climb revealed wonderful quilts, including these two quilts displayed on a pair of beds.

A walkway in Bath with the Minster or Cathedral spires looming in the background.

Whole cloth examples done by Elsie Walton, a student of Amy Emms.

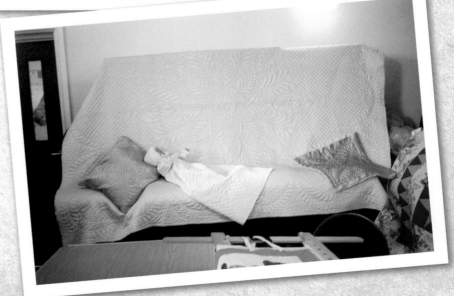

Wedgwood Quilt

48" x 48"

Who can think of England and blue and white and not think Wedgwood? On each trip to England I visit one of the factories that manufacture fine china. Royal Worcester in the city of Worcester is the closest to the site of the Quilts UK quilt show held each year in the merry month of May. The show site is the Three Counties Showground near Malvern in the midlands. It was my pleasure to judge Quilts UK in 1998. After the show I toddled off in my rental car to explore the many quaint towns and villages nearby. That marked my first foray into Wales where I stumbled upon the famous bookstore lined streets of Hay on Wye. It happened to be the weekend of their literary festival and the town was jammed with book lovers and visiting authors. One more happy adventure (because I had a car).

The preprinted panel used as the medallion center was a "gift" find at a local English guild's quilt show in 2008. Appropriately, the English manufacturer Makower produced the panel.

Ledbury Church sits just off the high street in this market town.

Yardage Requirements

» One preprinted panel or an 18" finished block of your choice
» 1/4 yard each of 6-8 medium blue prints, mixed scale
» 5/8 yard of medium blue print for piecing and inner frame
» 1/4 yard each of 6-8 light value blue on cream prints and light blue prints, mixed scale
» 4 yards blue on white toile or similar style print for final frame, binding, and backing
» 52" x 52" batting

Note: Fat quarters may be used but they will not cut as efficiently.

» From the 5/8 yard blue print, cut and set aside 1/4 yard for plain frame.
» From the toile, reserve a strip 20" x 50" for final frame. The backing will be pieced from the rest.

The center medallion is your preprinted panel or block or an 18" finished block of your choice.

Cutting and Construction

Frame 1:

Dogtooth

From assorted prints cut

» 6 - 4 1/4" squares from blue prints, subcut twice diagonally for 24 triangles
» 7 - 4 1/4" squares of blue on cream print, subcut twice diagonally for 28 triangles

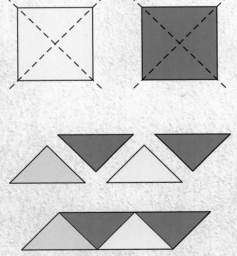

» Sew 6 blue and 7 cream or light blue print triangles to complete the Dogtooth strip: repeat for each frame. Add the side frames first, then the top and bottom frames. The corners are mitered.

Frame 2:

A plain frame

From the 5/8 yard blue print cut

- » 2 - 2" x 21 1/2" strips for the side frames
- » 2 - 2" x 24 1/32" strips for the top and bottom frames

Sew the side frames to center portion of the quilt and then add the top and bottom frames.

Frame 3:

Evening Stars

For each Evening Star block cut

- » 1 - 3 1/2" square blue print
- » 4 - 2 3/8" squares blue print, subcut once on the diagonal
- » 1 - 4 1/4" square cream print, subcut twice diagonally
- » 4 - 2 1/2" squares cream print

Repeat to make 20 Evening Star blocks of assorted prints.

Frame 4:

Dogtooth cut

- » 6 - 7 1/4" squares assorted medium blue prints, cut twice diagonally
- » 7 - 7 1/4" squares assorted cream and light blue prints, cut twice diagonally

*See Frame 1 art for construction, you will be using 7 1/4" squares for this frame.

- » Sew 6 blue and 7 cream or light blue print triangles for each Dogtooth frame. Attach the frames. The corners are mitered.

Frame 5:

Plain cut

» 4 - 4" x 48 3/4 Toile

This last frame is mitered. Sew the side frames, then the top and bottom. Miter the corners.

Assembly Diagram

Finishing

For the center panel and final frame quilting motifs, see pages 92-93.

Binding

Cut 6 strips 1 3/4" wide for binding. Join the strips for a continuous length of binding**. Fold the binding in half along the length and press. Attach the binding to the quilt edge using a 1/4" seam allowance, catching both cut sides. Miter at the corners. Turn to the back and slip stitch.

**Note: I join my binding strips diagonally so that the connecting seams are less visible.

Step onto the trolley at the Beamish Open Air Museum and be transported to the sights and sounds another era.

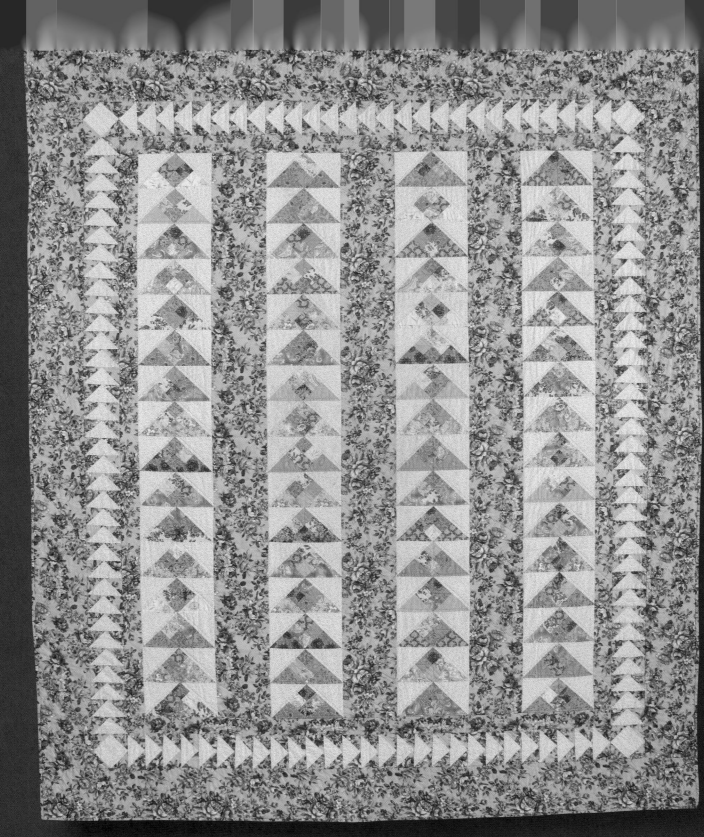

St. Ives Strippy Quilt

74" x 88"

You know the old riddle, "As I was going to St. Ives"? Well I found myself going to St. Ives-sort of. I was actually on my way to a village called Hemingford Grey not too far from Cambridge. St Ives just happened to be where I spent the night before going to the home of Lucy Boston. Lucy was a prominent patchworker. She took up patchwork fairly late in life but managed to make her mark anyway. She lived in a Norman built house, the oldest continuously privately occupied Norman house in Britain. Her daughter-in-law has the house open for tours so that the patchwork can be seen. Lucy also wrote a series of children's books about the *Children of Green Knowe*. The garden is full of topiary yew trees cut in shapes of crowns to mark the coronation of Elizabeth II. Visitors go to Lucy's house for all of these connections.

I named this quilt St Ives because it is so directional. If you follow the Flying Geese border you have a rough idea of my next day spent in Cambridge.

> As I was going to St. Ives
> I met a man with seven wives,
>
> Each wife had seven sacks,
> each sack had seven cats,
>
> Each cat had seven kits:
> kits, cats, sacks and wives,
>
> How many were going to St. Ives?

Yardage Requirements

- » 1/4 yard each of at least 12 assorted floral prints for the blocks in the pieced strips
- » 5 yards of chintz (large to medium scale floral) for sashing, frames, and binding
- » 3 yards light print for blocks and flying geese frame
- » 5 1/2 yards backing
- » 80" x 94" batting

Cutting

Note: cut the longest frames and panels first. **Templates are on pages 77-78.**

From assorted prints cut
- » 256 template A (It is important to use the template for A for best results.)
- » 32 - 5 1/4" squares, cut diagonally twice for a total of 128 triangles or 128 template B

From Chintz cut

For outer frame strips
- » 2 - 6 1/2" x 76 1/2"
- » 2 - 6 1/2" x 74 1/2"

For sashing strips cut
- » 3 - 6 1/2" x 64 1/2"

For inner frame strips cut
- » 2 - 2 1/2" x 64 1/2"
- » 2 - 2 1/2" x 54 1/2"

For binding cut
- » 8 - 2 1/2" x 42"

For flying geese frame cut
- » 130 - 2 7/8" squares, cut diagonally once for a total of 260 or 260 template D

From the light print cut
- » 64 - 4 7/8" squares, cut diagonally for a total of 128 triangles or 128 template C
- » 31 - 5 1/4" squares, cut diagonally twice for a total of 124 triangles or 122 template B
- » 4 - 3 3/8" squares or 4 template E for the corners of the flying geese frame.

Note: Using the template will give more accurate result.

Construction

Block unit

» Pieced unit in strips: For each unit you need 4 assorted floral squares from template A, 2 assorted floral triangles (B), and 2 light print triangles (C).

» Make a Four Patch of the assorted A squares, add B triangles of the same print to 2 sides as shown below. Note: your best results will come from using template A.

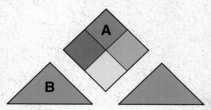

» Complete the unit by adding 2 Cs.

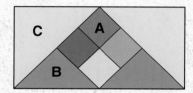

» Repeat unit construction for a total of 64 units. Each unit should measure 4 1/2" x 8 1/2" including seam allowances.

Assembling the rows of block units

» Sew 16 blocks together in 4 vertical rows or strips. Press the seam allowances in each row in one direction. Each row should measure 8 1/2" x 64 1/2".

Assembling the center panel of the quilt

» Mark 4" intervals on the chintz strips: cut the strips to be placed between the pieced units. This will align the alternate rows of pieced units. Sew the strips of pieced units alternating with chintz strips, use the marked 4" intervals to keep the pieced units aligned. Press the seam allowances toward the chintz strips. The center panel should measure 50 1/2" x 64 1/2" including seam allowances.

Add the inner frames

» Sew a 64 1/2" to each side of the center panel. Press toward chintz. Add a 54 1/2" frame to each end (top and bottom). Press toward the chintz frame.

Assembling the Flying Geese Frames

For each Flying Geese unit:

» Sew the long side of a chintz D triangle to each short side of a light print B.

» Repeat to make 122 Flying Geese units. Each unit should measure 4 1/2" x 2 1/2" including seam allowances.

For the side Flying Geese frame
» Sew 34 Flying Geese units together vertically. The strips should measure 4 1/2" x 68 1/2" each. Sew the side Flying Geese frame to each side of the quilt center.

For the corner units of the Flying Geese frame
» Sew a floral chintz triangle D to each side of the light print square E. Repeat for the 4 corners.

For the top and bottom Flying Geese frame:
» Sew 27 Flying Geese units together in a strip; add a corner unit to each end. The top and bottom Flying Geese frames should measure 4 1/2" x 62 1/2".
» Sew Flying Geese frame to top and bottom of the quilt center. Now the center should measure 62 1/2" x 76 1/2".

Add the final chintz frame
» Sew a 6 1/2" x 76 1/2" chintz floral to each side of the quilt center. Add a 6 1/2" x 74 1/2" to the top and bottom of the quilt.

Finishing

» To avoid a mid-line seam on the back, split one 2 3/4 yard section in half lengthwise and sew to each side of the other 2 3/4 yard section. Some additional quilting motifs that are suitable for the long plain strips are on pages 87, 93 and 95.

Binding

» Cut 10 - 2" strips form the theme fabric, join the strips diagonally. Fold lengthwise and press. Sew to the right side of the quilt using a 1/4" seam allowance. Turn to the back and slip stitch.

Assembly Diagram

LIMERICK MEDALLION QUILT

68 1/4" x 68 1/4"

Ireland is a magical country. I fell in love on my first visit and will go back as often as given a chance. Limerick is the first city I visited. I taught workshops in an Irish quilt shop and made new friends every day. One of those new friends, Emer Fahy, is completing a doctorate with emphasis on quilts in Ireland and provided photos of quilts. One of those quilts is in part the inspiration for Limerick Medallion. The green and lavender palette harkens back to the lush colors I saw.

YARDAGE REQUIREMENTS

- » 3 1/2 yards focus or theme print, medium to large scale
- » 1/2 yard each of 6-8 prints-color 1 (mixers) values should range from medium to very dark
- » 1/2 yard each of 6-8 prints-color 2 (mixers) values should range from medium to very dark
- » 1/2 yard of primary background fabric (for Mariner's Compass and mixers)
- » 1/2 each of 6-8 background prints
- » 3/4 yard dark print for binding
- » 4 1/4 yards backing
- » 72" x 72" batting

***Note:** Before cutting into the focus/theme fabric, set 2 yards aside for frames 6 and 8.

An Irish frame quilt top. This quilts features many of the traditional elements in both English and Irish frame quilts. Photos by Emer Fahy.

This Irish frame quilt helped set the color palette for Limerick Medallion. It reflects the soft greens and lavenders of the Irish countryside.

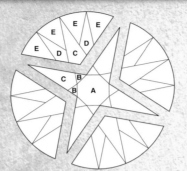 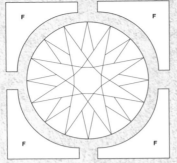 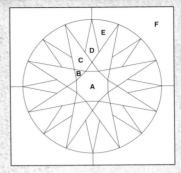

Mariner's Compass

Construction

Mariner's Compass:

16" finished (16 1/2" with seam allowance)

» You need one medium=M, 1 dark=D, and 1 very dark=VD from color group 1. Be sure there is contrast between the values.
» You also need your primary background fabric=L.
» Use the templates for the Mariner's Compass on page 79-80.

Cut

» 1 – color D from template A
» 8 – color VD from template B
» 8 – color D from template C
» 8 – color M from template D
» 16 - background L template E
» 4 - background L template F

Cutting and Construction

Note: Cut and reserve all the frame strips before using any of the theme fabric for piecing. Reserve 3/4 of a yard for binding.

Mariner's Compass:

» Join all Bs to the center A (see example, right).
» Inset 4 C pieces at the north, south, east and west compass points.
» Set the center aside and construct 4 pie-shaped wedges, joining Es to either side of Ds. Join these D/E wedges to either side of the remaining C pieces.
» Inset these C/D/E wedges into the compass center section.
» Attach the background Fs pieces as shown (right).

Frame 1:

A plain fabric frame: Cut from theme/focus fabric

» 2 - 3" x 16 1/2" strips for top and bottom frames

- » 2 - 3" x 21 1/2" strips for side frames
- » Cut these strips on the width of the fabric.
- » Attach top and bottom frames first, then the side frames.

Frame 2:

Framed squares
- » You need 32 framed squares for this frame.

Cut
- » 32 - 3 1/2" squares from theme fabric
- » 128 - 2" squares, assorted from the group of background fabrics

Begin with a 3 1/2" square and 4 - 2" squares. With right sides together, stitch a square along its diagonal to each corner of the 3 1/2" square. Trim away the excess at each corner and press. You can make opposite diagonals before trimming and pressing.

Repeat the process for the other 2 corners. Trim away excess and press. The framed square created will have a finished size of 3". Your finished framed square units will create the framed squares.

Frame 3:

A plain frame for focus/theme fabric, cut
- » 4 - 3" x 27 1/2" focus/theme fabric
- » 4 - 3" squares from color 2, all 4 alike

Sew a 3" square to each end of the remaining 2 strips (sides of frame 3). Align the corner squares with the top and bottom frames and sew on the side frames.

Frame 4:

Triple Squares, cut
- » 180 - assorted mixers, 60 from color 1, 60 from color 2 and 60 from backgrounds.
- » 34 - 3 1/2" squares backgrounds, subcut on both diagonals for 136 quarter-square triangles. The more variety throughout, the better.
- » You need 60 triple-square sections and 4 corners or turning units.
- » Each side of the quilt requires 15 triple-square units sewn together plus a corner or turning unit to complete that frame.

For the corner units cut

- » 4 - 2" squares color 2
- » 12 - 2" squares color 1.
- » 6 - 3 1/2" background squares, subcut on both diagonals.

Make the rows of triple squares so the color 1s align, backgrounds in the middle and color 2s align.

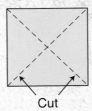

Cut

Subcut 3 1/2" squares diagonally twice.

Each unit consists of a triangle 3 - 2" squares and another triangle.
Stitch the unit together.

Align the units as shown, offsetting by 1 square. Stitch together. Trim edges if needed —
the finished strip should be 4 3/4" wide.

Turning unit construction. This unit completes the frame.

Triple-squares unit with the turning unit added.

Frame 5:

Sawtooth, cut

» 32 - 3 1/2" squares, subcut once on the diagonal of assorted mixers, color 1
» 32 - 3 1/2" squares, subcut once on the diagonal of assorted mixers, color 2.

You need 64 Sawtooth units.

Subcut squares into 2 half-square triangles. Stitch the triangles together along the diagonal; avoid stretching as you stitch.

Sawtooth units will measure 3 1/8" unfinished.

Sew 15 Sawtooth units together for the top and bottom frames and 17 Sawtooth units for the side frames. Attach the top and bottom frames first, then attach the side frames.

Frame 6:

Plain fabric, cut

» 4 - 3 1/4" x 46 3/4" strips focus/theme fabric
» 4 - 3 1/4" squares

Attach the top and bottom frames first, then sew a square to each end of the remaining side frames strips. Attach the side frames.

Frame 7:

Dogtooth, cut

» 7 - 9 1/4" squares focus/theme fabric, subcut on both diagonals to make 28 quarter-square triangles.

» 8 - 9 1/4" squares from one of the prints in the color 2 group. Subcut on both diagonals to make 32 quarter-square triangles.

You need 4 frame groups, each with 7 triangles from focus/theme and 8 from 1 of color group 2.

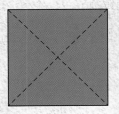

Subcut the 6 1/2" squares diagonally twice.

Stitch together as shown.

Frame 8:

Plain plus a four patch at corners, cut
» 4 - 5" x 57" from the focus/theme fabric

For the Four Patch at the corners cut
» 8 - 2 3/4" squares from the focus/theme fabric.
» 8 - 2 3/4" squares from color 2 fabric, the same as in the Dogtooth frame.

Piece the Four Patches.

Attach the top and bottom frames. Sew a Four Patch to each end of the remaining frame strips and attach to the quilt.

Assembly Diagram

Finishing

Some quilting motifs are on pages 95-96.

Cut 8 strips 2" wide across the width for binding from the binding fabric. Join the strips for a continuous length of binding**. Fold the binding in half along the length and press. Attach the binding to the quilt edge using a 1/4" seam allowance, catching both cut sides. Miter at the corners. Turn to the back and slip stitch.

**Note: I join my binding strips diagonally so that the connecting seams are less visible.

See pages 79-80 for the templates.

Victorian Etui

Size: about 3 1/2" x 3 1/2" x 4 1/2"

An Etui is a folding portable sewing kit. These Victorian style needle boxes were made by ladies but were also made by soldiers and seaman in the 19th century. They were used up to and during World War I. I saw many examples of these in a display case at the Needle Forge Museum in Reddich.

Supply list

» 3/8 yard fabric for outside and inside towers of etui
» 1/8 yard of fabric for inside of towers
» 1 1/2 yards of 3/8" wide ribbon (includes ribbon for top)
» 1/2 yard of poly fleece or 24" x 24" batting
» 1/2 yard Heat 'n Bond or a fusible of your choice

Note: using a fusible saves lots of gluing, but glue pieces if you prefer.

» A fist full of fiberfill (or use batting)
» 1 (~18" x 26") piece of heavy posterboard or crescent board (a heavy cardboard) - both are available at art and craft stores
» Masking tape
» Tacky glue
» A ruler with a metal edge or something that you can use to score the cardboard
» *Optional:* lace or trim to decorate the top of the Etui. You need about 5/8 yard of trim to go around the top edge of the top. Add shells, buttons or tassels to suit your taste.

Put whatever you want inside…sewing needles, pins, small scissors, a thimble, and assorted notions.

Cut the board as directed on the pattern pieces. Cut the board on the solid lines and score for folding on the dotted lines.

From the ribbon cut

» 4 - 4 1/2" pieces
» 4 - 2 1/4" pieces
» 1 - 5" piece for the pull
» 1 - 17" piece for trim on cover

From fleece or batting cut these pieces

- » 1 - 1" x 1"
- » 4 - 3 1/2" x 3 1/8" for outer tower flaps
- » 2 - 3 5/8" x 3 5/8" for the top
- » 4 - 2 3/4" x 1 1/4" for inner tower flaps

From outer fabric cut (pattern pieces are on pages 81-85)

- » 1 - outer tower A, 1" larger all the way around the board size: cut fusible to match size
- » 1 - inside tower B, 1" larger all the way around: cut fusible to match size
- » 1 – base C, 4 7/8" x 4 7/8" and fusible to match size
- » 1 cover D, 1" larger than the inside: cut fusible to match size
- » 2 - cover inserts I, 4 5/8" x 4 5/8"
- » 1 - 1" larger all around than thimble holder piece G

From inside fabric cut

- » 4 - 4 1/2" x 4 1/2"
- » 4 - 3 3/4" x 2 1/4"

Construction

- » Fuse fabric A, B, C, and D to the corresponding fusible for those pieces. Wrap extra fabric around the edges and fuse or glue.
- » Place board A on the fusible side of fabric A and fuse into place. Wrap the additional fabric around and fuse to the edges, securing any loose edges with glue.

- » Cut 1 - 5" x 5" (check that this cut size will cover the inside base of the outer tower A so that the cardboard doesn't show) from the outer fabric. Glue this piece, right side up, to the center of A, covering the board as shown.

» Cover board C and wrap the extra fabric around the edges, fuse or glue in place. Glue the covered piece C to the bottom of the outer tower as shown.

» Glue fleece/batting to the flaps (E) of the outer tower. Place fleece/batting side face down on the wrong side of the 4 1/2" squares of lining fabric. Wrap the fabric around to back side and secure with glue. Repeat for all 4 flaps.

» Place 1 - 4 1/2" piece of ribbon over the covered flaps, about 1 7/8" from the end. Glue the ends securely to the back side of the flaps.

» Repeat these steps for the inner tower piece B, using a 2 1/4" square centered on the inner tower base as you did for the outer tower base E

» Place 2 1/4" ribbon about 1 7/8" from 1 end of each flap. Glue the ribbon ends securely to the back side of flaps.

» Place the inner tower diagonally as shown. Glue securely to the outer tower.

Thimble Holder

» Fuse the fabric cover for the thimble cover G in place. Fold the thimble holder on the scored lines to form a box. Tape the side and bottom with masking tape.

» Glue any excess fabric to cover the edges. Glue fleece to the thimble cover board top to form a box and cover with lining fabric as you did for flaps.

» Glue the top to the thimble holder top flap. Fill thimble tower 2/3 full with batting. Cut a small piece of fabric, about 1 1/2" square and tuck it into the sides to cover and hide the batting.

» Glue the thimble holder to the center of the inner tower.

Etui top

- » The top is piece D covered with outer fabric. Fold it on the scored lines. Glue fleece/batting to the insert for the top (piece 'I') and cover with lining fabric as you did for the tower flaps.
- » Make the hinge by cutting a piece of outer fabric 2 1/4" x 4 1/2". Fold in the raw edges and glue to make a 4 1/2" hinge. Insert the hinge into the center back of the top as you glue the insert into place. Leave approximately 3" of the hinge free.
- » Insert a 5" piece of ribbon, folded in half lengthwise to form a loop, into the center front. Leave about 1" free. Glue the insert inside the top.
- » Glue the fleece/batting to piece 'I' and cover it with outer fabric for the padded top of the Etui. Glue to the top.
- » Holding the scored folded edges of the top in place, add the 17" piece of ribbon. Glue the ribbon around the top to hold the folded edges.
- » Place the Etui top on the base. Position the fabric hinge using a pencil to add slack. Glue the hinge to the back of the outer tower.
- » You can embellish the top as desired with buttons, beads, shells, or lace.
- » Fill your Etui with your choice of sewing notions. Slide needle packs, scissors, etc. into the ribbons on the padded towers.

Places to See and Events

The Forge Mill Needle Museum, Reddich England, Needle Mill Lane, Redditch, Worcester B98 8HY, phone: 011 44 1527 62509 www.forgemill. org.uk Here you can see the process that produces virtually all the needles we use. Forge Mill Needle Museum in Redditch is an unusual and fascinating place to visit. This historic site illustrates the rich heritage of the needle and fishing tackle industries. Models and recreated scenes provide a vivid illustration of how needles were once made, and how Redditch once produced 90 percent of the world's needles.

Forge Mill Needle Museum

The Manor, Hemingfor Grey Huntingdon PE18 9BN, Phone: 011 44 1480 463134

http://www.greenknowe.co.uk. This is the home of Lucy Boston.

» Built in the 1130s The Manor is one of the oldest continuously inhabited houses in Britain. Much of the original house remains virtually intact in spite of various changes over nine hundred years. The upstairs hall is a room full of atmosphere and the echoes of nearly nine centuries of family conversations. It was used during World War II by Lucy Boston to give gramophone record recitals twice a week to the RAF. The 1929 EMG gramophone is still in use in this room. Email: diana_boston@ hotmail.com

A quilt in the Lucy Boston home.

Photo by Diana Boston.

Bowes Museum, Barnard Castle, County Durham DL12 8NP, phone: 011 44 1833 690606, http://www.thebowesmuseum.org.uk

Jinney Ring Craft Centre, Hanbury, Nr Bromsgrove, Worcester, B60 4BU, phone: 011 44 1527 821272, http://www.jinneyringcraft.co.uk

Victoria and Albert Museum, V&A South Kensington Cromwell Road London SW7 2RL011 44 20 7942 2000, http://www.vam.ac.uk

Quarry Bank Mill and Styal Estate, Styal, Wimslow, Cheshire SK9 4LA, UK phone: 011 44 1625 527468, http://www.nationaltrust.org.uk

- » Mill owner's picturesque private garden
- » The most powerful working waterwheel in Europe
- » Practical demonstrations in the mill
- » Discover the effects of the Industrial Revolution on how we lived and worked
- » Woodland and riverside walks provide a tranquil contrast

The American Museum in Britain, Claverton Manor, Bath, BA2 7BD, phone: 011 44 1225 460503, www.americanmuseum.org

- » The American Museum at Bath has an extensive collection of American Quilts. From time to time they have special exhibitions of quilts from other than their own collections

Beamish Open Air Museum, Beamish Museum Limited Regional Resource Centre County Durham DH9 0RG, UK, phone: 011 44 0191 370 4000 http://www.beamish.org.uk/

The Quilters' Guild of The British Isles Museum, St Anthony's Hall York, YO1 7PW, UK, phone: 011 44 1904 613242, http://www.quiltersguild.org.uk

This whole cloth red wool quilt lies on a bed in Bunratty Castle, just outside of Limerick Ireland.

Events

I love Quilts UK usually held the third week and weekend in May at Severn Hall, Three Counties Showground, Malvern, Worcestershire. This is a favorite of quiltmakers in the UK, known as the friendly show. Other shows produced by Grosvenor can be found along with Quilts UK at http://www.grosvenorexhibitions.co.uk and link to Quilts UK.

Festival of Quilts, held at the NEC, Birmingham, The Festival of Quilts (organized with the support of the Quilters Guild of the British Isles) has earned a reputation over the past five years as the largest, most inspiring quilting event in Europe - with good reason!

http://www.twistedthread.com

Suggested Resources

Allen, Rosemary E. *North Country Quilts and Coverlets from the Beamish Museum*. County Durham: Beamish Museum, 1987

Allen, Rosemary E. *Quilts and Coverlets. The Beamish Collection*. Beamish, The North of England Open Air Museum. 2007

Averil, Colby. *Patchwork Quilts*. 1965. Reprint, London: B.T. Batsford Lt., 1988

Fitzrandolph, Mavis. *Traditional Quilting, Its Story and Practice*. London, Batsford, 1954

Jen Jones, *Welsh Quilts*, Quiltmania, 2005

Meldrum, Alex, Curator. *Irish Patchwork*, Kilkenny, Ireland. Design Workshop Ltd. 1979. An exhibition catalog

Osler, Dorothy. *North Country Quilts*. Friends of the Bowes Museum, 2000

Osler, Dorothy. *Traditional British Quilts*. London, Batsford Ltd. 1987

Quilt Treasures of Great Britain: The Heritage Search of the Quilters' Guild. Rutledge Hill Press, 1985

Rae, Janet. *The Quilts of the British Isles*. E. P. Dutton, 1987

Osler, Dorothy. *Quilting Design Sourcebook*, That Patchwork Place, 1996

A pedestrian view of the river through the city of Bath. The open park area skirts the bustle of the thoroughfare.

A market house in Ledbury is an important feature of a 'market town', towns that host farm-to-market goods on a regular schedule.

Hedgerows line the streets of Adair, sheltering the buildings for privacy.

Each year the awards for all categories of Quilts UK competition were awarded on the final day of the show. The special guest to make the presentations in 1998 was Amy Emms. Amy passed away three weeks later.

A manufacturer panel designed for frame quilts in the early 19th century.

This pastoral scene is just off the garden of my good friend Dianne Huck. When I visited England, Dianne's home called Oak Tree Cottage has been a lovely place to stay.

TEMPLATES
AND
QUILTING
MOTIFS

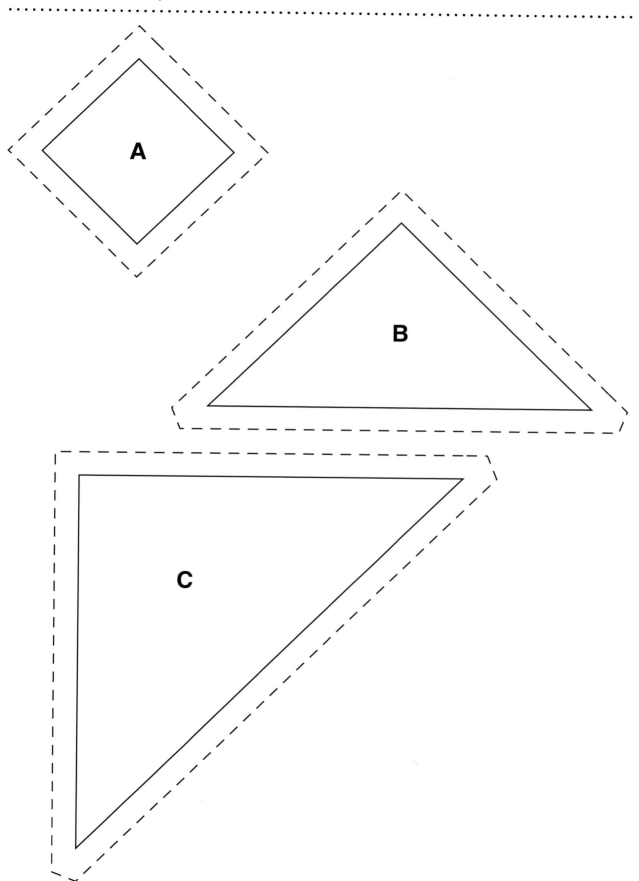

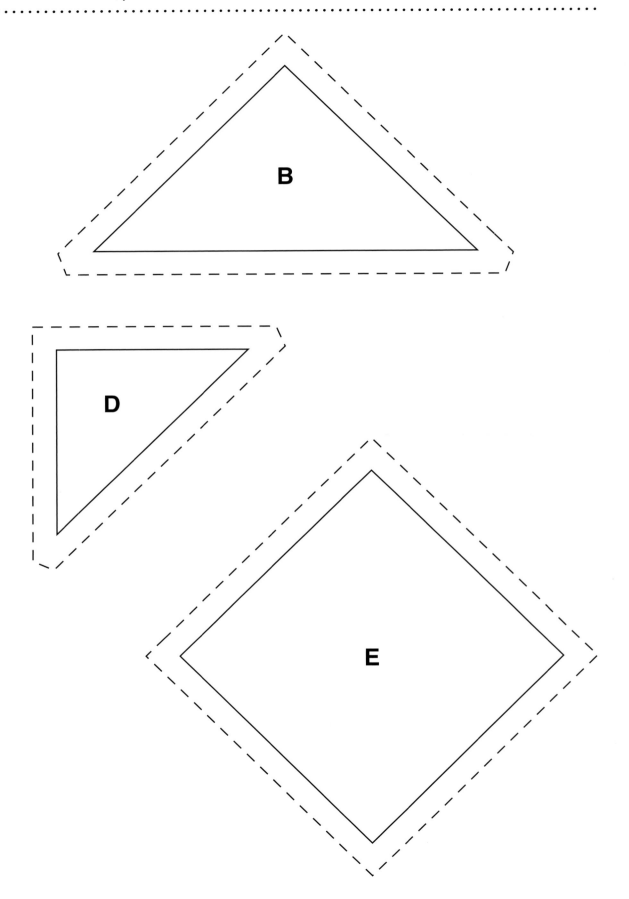

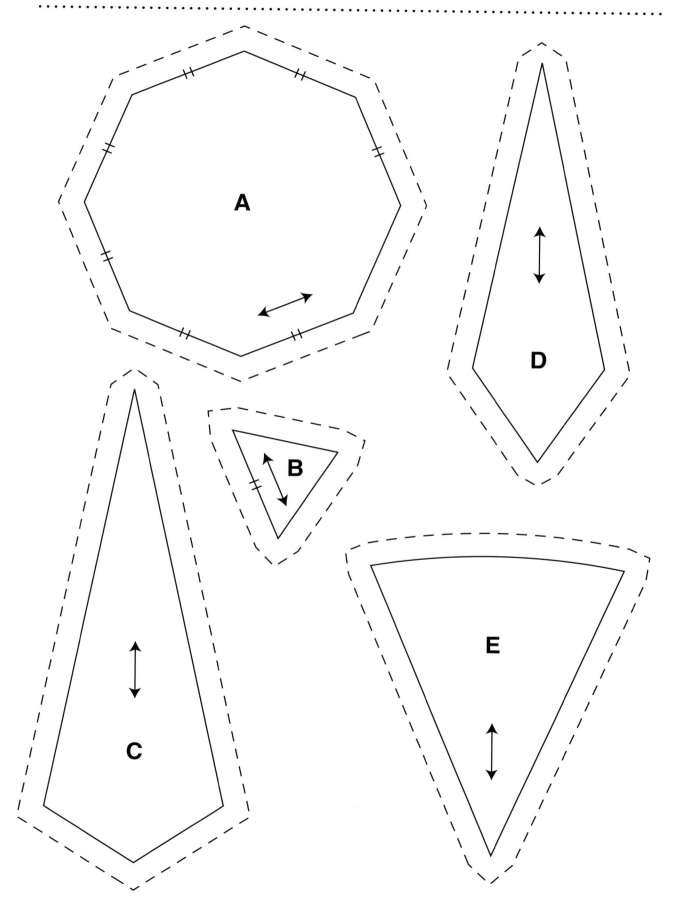

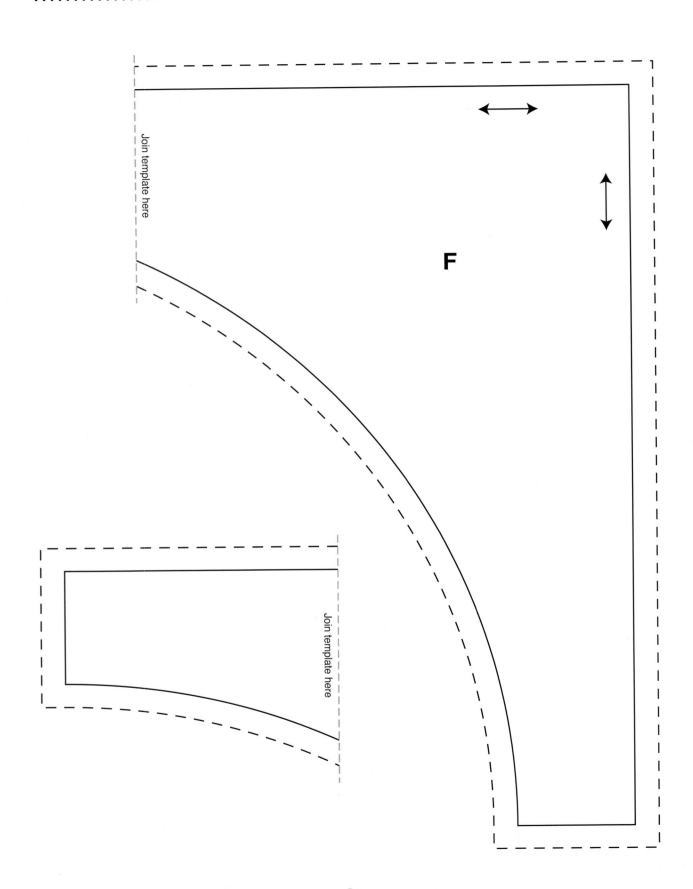

Join template here

F

Join template here

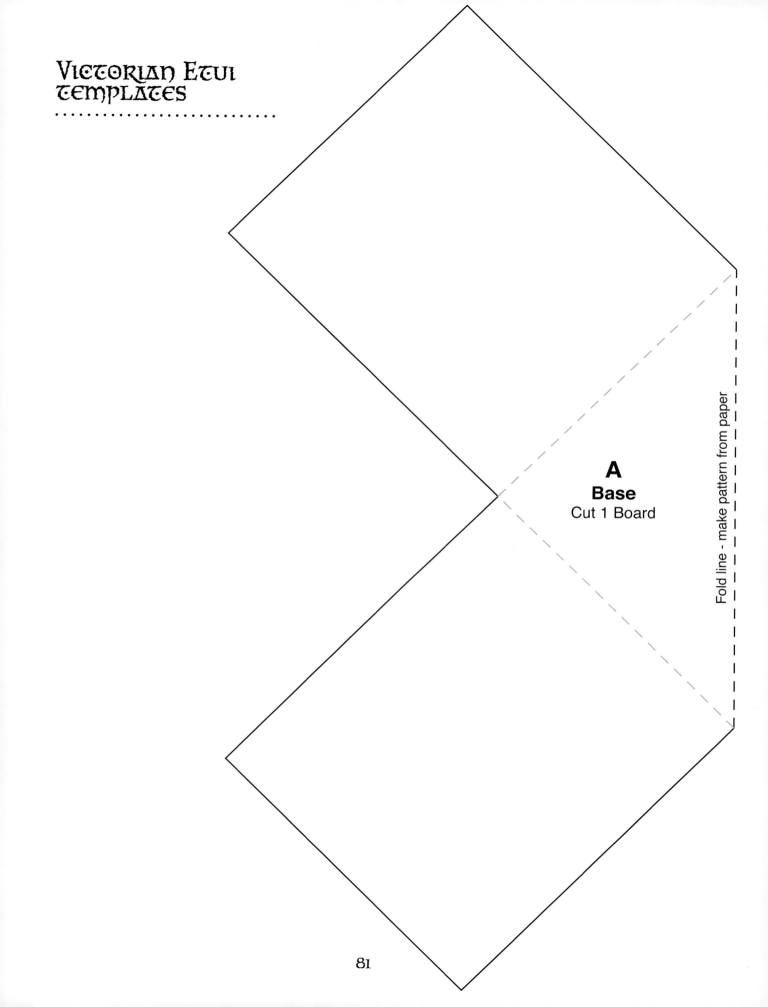

Victorian Etui
Templates

A
Base
Cut 1 Board

Fold line - make pattern from paper

B
Inside
Cut 1 Board

C
Bottom
Cut 1 Board

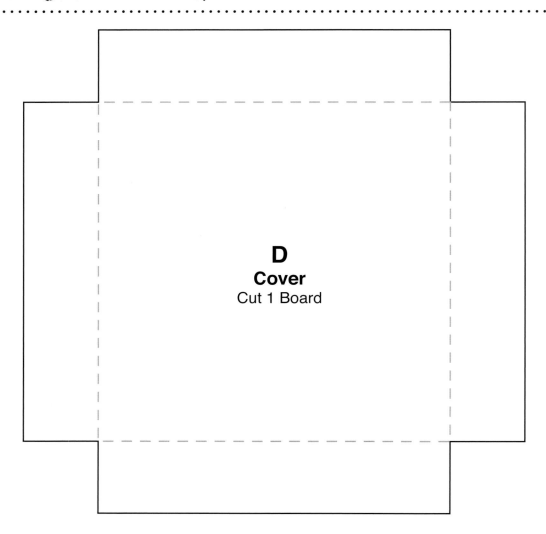

D
Cover
Cut 1 Board

E
Base Flaps
Cut 4 Boards &
Fleece or Batting

F
Inside Flap
Cut 4 Boards
& Fleece or
Batting

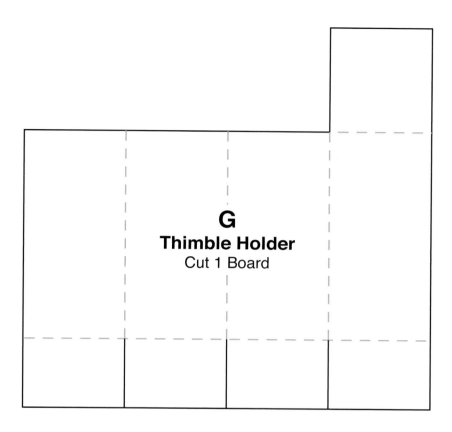

G
Thimble Holder
Cut 1 Board

I
Cover Insert
Cut 2 Boards & Fleece

H
Thimble Top
Cut 1 Board
& Fleece

Quilting Your Quilt

S everal traditional patterns used on British Isles quilts are included in the following pages. Dorothy Olser's work on documenting the quilts, including the quilting patterns, was an invaluable aid. You'll note there isn't a pattern for every quilt or area on a quilt. The quiltmakers relied heavily on straight-line grids and fill patterns (patterns used to fill in vacant areas behind motifs).

I used many of those options on the quilts in this book. I could avoid unnecessary marking by making use of various sizes of masking tape to lay on the grids. Quilting on the bias of the fabrics is also helpful because the fabric flexes more on the bias and makes it easier to needle.

Please feel free to use the motifs provided on any of the quilts and in any areas that fit. Make the choice of quilting motifs based on what you want on your quilt.

Beamish Strippy: Align on both center striped panels. This motif may also be used in other long frames or borders at least 5-6" wide.

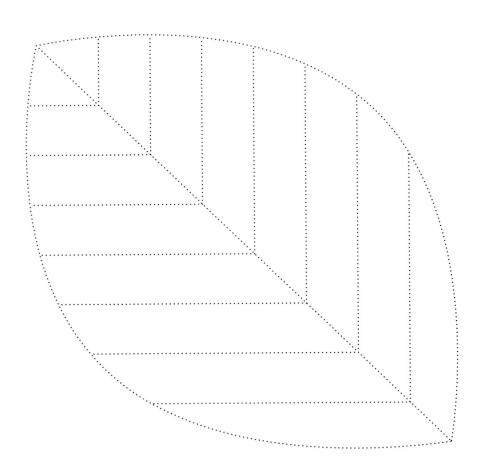

Abergavenny Welsh: Align the spirals on the grey frame. Spirals similar to this motif are an important quilting element in Welsh quilting. The leaf motif is placed diagonally in the black, blue and red corners. Design digitized from the original quilt by Christy Gray – Katydid Design Studio.

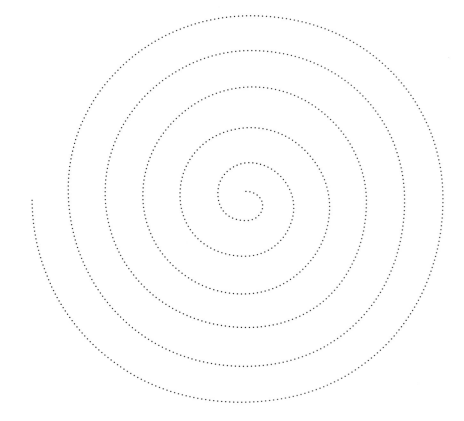

A Nod to Amy: Individual center spirals, called Scissors. They are a commonly used motif in Durham traditional quilting.

Arrangement of individual center spirals on A Nod to Amy. Even though a single Scissor motif is shown, scissors are most often found arranged in this circular array. For the complete design, the 'scissors' should be arranged in a circle using 8 repeats of the motif. Use a 3 3/4" circle guide as the center and fold the fabric into eighths to get the 8 guide lines. Place the Scissors motif as shown using the eighth folds lines as the center line of the Scissors.

Bildeston Uneven Nine Patch: Knotted circle - place in alternate blocks. This Celtic style pattern adapted from Quilting Design Sourcebook *by Dorothy Osler. Bildeston Uneven Nine Patch: This motif, adapted from the Knotted Circle, fills the half-square triangles on the outer edge of the quilt.*

Use notches for placement

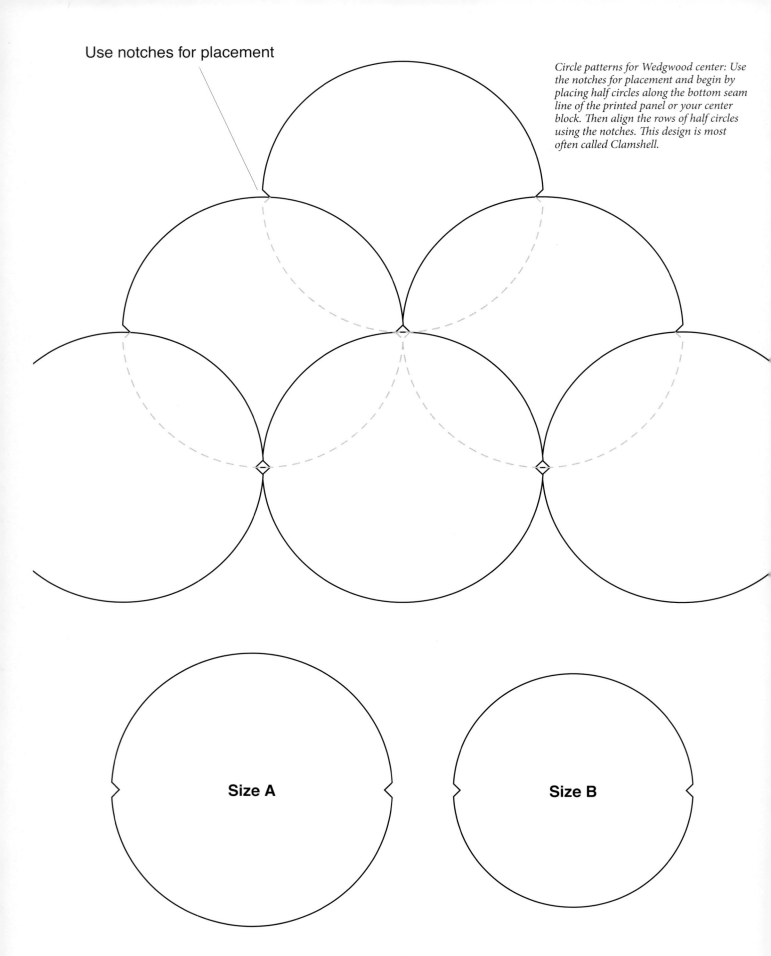

Circle patterns for Wedgwood center: Use the notches for placement and begin by placing half circles along the bottom seam line of the printed panel or your center block. Then align the rows of half circles using the notches. This design is most often called Clamshell.

Size A

Size B

Wedgwood: Place this motif in the final frame of the quilt, starting at the corner and continuing to overlap the design to make it flow. Stop about halfway and begin at the next corner, then come back to meet the knot at the center. (this may required some adjustment as the knots connect.

This Quadrafoil quilting motif may be used in any 5"-6" square as a fill.

Limerick Medallion: This simple shallow tapered S can be manipulated into the narrow plain frames. Just be sure that the motifs overlap slightly. Use it in the narrow frames of Limerick but it may also be used in the narrow frames of Berrington Hall in the place of grid lines.

Limerick Medallion: This fan motif is placed on the seamlines of the Dogtooth frame.

Limerick Medallion: Use this cable design in the final frame. Overlap the oval for each repeat, begin at the corners and work toward the center. Flip for opposite corners.